ANIMALS ATTACK!

Wolves

Elizabeth J. Scholl

**KIDHAVEN
PRESS**™

THOMSON

™

GALE

San Diego • Detroit • New York • San Francisco • Cleveland
New Haven, Conn. • Waterville, Maine • London • Munich

THOMSON

GALE

© 2003 by KidHaven Press. KidHaven Press is an imprint of The Gale Group, Inc.,
a division of Thomson Learning, Inc.

KidHaven™ and Thomson Learning™ are trademarks used herein under license.

For more information, contact
KidHaven Press
27500 Drake Rd.
Farmington Hills, MI 48331-3535
Or you can visit our Internet site at http://www.gale.com

LIBRARY OF CONGRESS CATALOGING-IN-PUBLICATION DATA

Scholl, Elizabeth J.
  Wolves / by Elizabeth J. Scholl.
    v. cm. — (Animals attack!)
  Contents: A history of wolf attacks — Wolf attacks in North America — Child-
lifting wolves in India — Wolf hybrids—pets or killers?
  Includes bibliographical references (p.).
    ISBN 0-7377-1527-8 (hardback : alk. paper)
    1. Wolf attacks—Juvenile literature. [1. Wolves. 2. Animals attack!.] I. Title.
  II. Series.
    QL737.C22S354 2003
    599.773'1566
                                                            2002153394

Printed in China

Contents

Chapter 1

A History of Wolf Attacks

Most people are afraid of wolves. In fact, the wolf may be the first animal many children are taught to fear. Wolves haunt fairy tales and fables. In stories such as "Little Red Riding Hood," "The Three Little Pigs," and "The Boy Who Cried Wolf," wolves are sneaky, bloodthirsty animals.

Wolves also are portrayed poorly in common expressions. "Wolfing down your food" means eating in a very fast, greedy manner. "A wolf in sheep's clothing" describes a person who looks friendly but is, in fact, someone who is waiting to do harm.

Wolves have long been feared and hated. This dates back to when European settlers first arrived in

America. Wolves once roamed most areas of the United States, hunting buffalo, elk, and deer. As settlers moved west, they killed many of the large game animals on which wolves naturally fed. With fewer wild animals to prey upon, wolves began to hunt the cattle and sheep that belonged to the settlers. Wolves were regarded as enemies. People feared they would kill their livestock and attack their families.

An aggressive wolf snarls, showing its long sharp fangs.

"Wolfers" surround a pack of wolves and foxes. Wolves were nearly extinct in the United States by the 1950s.

The government began to offer rewards, or **bounties**, to people who killed wolves. People who hunted wolves were called **wolfers**. Wolves were hunted more, and the **prey** they usually hunted became harder to find. Wolves almost became **extinct** in the lower forty-eight states by the 1950s.

Attacks Are Rare

Today wolves rarely attack humans. When it has happened in North America, the attacks have occurred mostly in Canada and Alaska. Attacks usually involve children, though a few adults have also been attacked. Many reported attacks reveal that a single, or lone, wolf was responsible. Normally, wolves hunt in packs. A lone wolf may be sick or may have been rejected by its **pack** for some reason.

Wolves tend to live in areas far from large human population centers. In the forty-eight continental United States, there are only about three thousand wolves. Most wolves live in Minnesota, but small numbers also live in Michigan, Wisconsin, Montana, Idaho, and Wyoming. Alaska has a larger wolf population than all the other states combined, having between six thousand and eight thousand wolves.

A pack of timber wolves tears into a deer carcass.

Canada, home to fifty to sixty thousand wolves, has one of the largest wolf populations in the world.

Russia and Mongolia have the second-largest wolf populations, each having thirty thousand wolves. China has about six thousand wolves, and India's wolf population is somewhere between two thousand and three thousand. Spain is home to one of the larger European wolf populations, with about two thousand wolves. Italy has somewhere around four hundred wolves, and Greece has two hundred to three hundred wolves. Wolves are extinct in many European countries.

During the 1700s and 1800s, wolf attacks occurred in France, Russia, Sweden, Finland, Norway, and Italy. In one area of France, called Gévaudan, over one hundred people were killed in the three-year period between 1764 and 1767. The two animals responsible are believed to have been wolf dogs.

Why Wolves Attack

Wolves attack for a variety of reasons. The majority of reported wolf attacks throughout history have been by wolves with **rabies**. Attacks by **rabid** wolves have been recorded as far back as 1557 and as recently as 2001. Rabies among wolves has decreased greatly during the twentieth century in North America and western Europe, but it still remains a problem in other areas of the world. Other diseases, such as distemper and parovirus, can also affect wolves' behavior.

A wolf may attack if it feels it is in danger of being attacked or if it believes its **den** is being attacked,

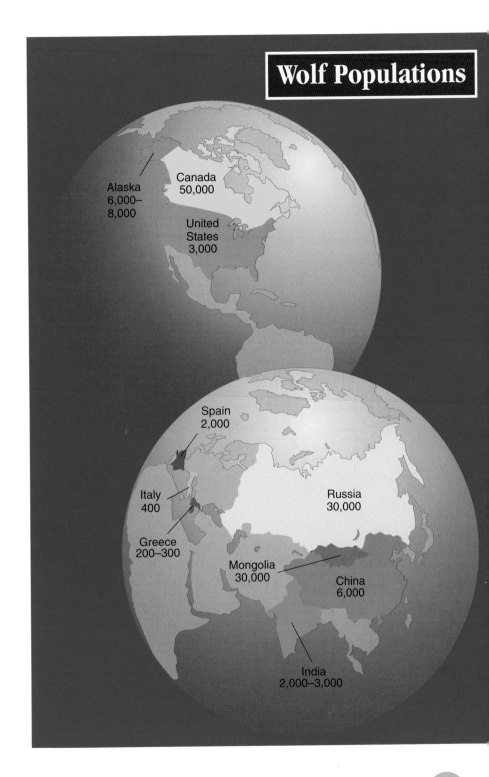

Wolf Populations

Alaska
6,000–
8,000

Canada
50,000

United
States
3,000

Spain
2,000

Italy
400

Greece
200–300

Russia
30,000

Mongolia
30,000

China
6,000

India
2,000–3,000

Habituated wolves, like this wolf in Yellowstone National Park, have been known to attack humans.

particularly if there are pups in the den. If a wolf is trapped or cornered, it also may attack.

Attacks by wolves hunting down humans as food are the most rare types of attacks. These are known as **predatory attacks**. Humans are not natural prey for wolves. Predatory attacks usually happen when a wolf is extremely hungry, or starving. For example, in Iran in 1997 a four-year-old boy was killed and partially eaten by a starving wolf. The wolf picked up the boy from the courtyard of his home.

Habituation

Another factor in wolf attacks is **habituation**—that is, when wolves lose their fear of humans. In recent years this has become more common and is a dangerous situation. Habituated wolves become bolder around humans and look for food where humans live or camp. Habituated wolves have been known to attack the people with whom they come in contact.

In August 1996 in Ontario, Canada, while camping with his family, a twelve-year-old boy was pulled from his sleeping bag by a wolf. The boy survived, but he had serious wounds on his head and face, where the wolf had grabbed him. The wolf that attacked him had been habituated to humans. Before the attack, it had been seen taking items such as sneakers and backpacks from campsites in the area.

Another incident of a wolf attacking children was reported in rural China in 1992. A wolf grabbed two young sisters in its jaws. The girls' mother attacked the wolf with a **sickle** and fought with the wolf until other people came and drove the wolf away, saving the children.

Perhaps the most horrible and tragic reports of recent wolf attacks come from a village in northern

India in 1996. From March to October, seventy-six children were attacked by wolves. More than fifty of these children were killed. Man-eating wolves are extremely rare, but in this case, the circumstances were very unusual. The wolves in this area of India live close to an area with many people but few prey animals. Likewise, many small children are allowed to wander by themselves outdoors while their parents are working.

Wolves are fierce **predators**. They are wild animals capable of attacking and tearing apart a large animal or a human being. Although attacks are rare, wolves need to be respected as potentially dangerous.

Chapter 2

Wolf Attacks in North America

Because so many wolves live in Canada, most of the wolf attacks in North America occur there. It is estimated that fifty to sixty thousand wolves live in Canada, which is the largest wolf population of any country in the world today.

At least five wolf attacks in recent years have occurred in Algonquin Provincial Park, located in Ontario, Canada. The park attracts sixty thousand visitors each year. One of the reasons people visit Algonquin Park is for the chance to see a wolf in the wild. Park officials claim that more people have had **firsthand** experiences with wolves in Algonquin Park than in any other place in the world.

The thick forest of Algonquin Provincial Park (pictured) is home to large numbers of wild wolves.

Zacariah's Wolf Experience

Many Algonquin Park visitors come and go without seeing a wolf. This is because wolves are normally shy and because Algonquin Park is a thickly forested area. Those who get to see wolves usually feel very fortunate. Twelve-year-old Zacariah Delventhal had a different feeling about his experience with a wolf.

Zacariah and his family were camping in Algonquin Park during the summer of 1996. On their last night of a ten-day camping trip, Zacariah's family decided to sleep outside their tents, under the stars.

That night, while Zacariah was dreaming about walking in the woods, he awoke to a feeling of something pressing on his head. He had been dragged six feet. He yelled to his parents, "Something bit me!" When he asked his father what it was, his answer was, "A wolf."[1]

Five days after the attack, authorities shot and killed a sixty-pound male wolf, which was believed to be Zacariah's attacker. It was judged to be healthy,

A park official removes a wolf that was shot after it attacked a park visitor.

Long skull supports a large brain, and acts as an anchor for powerful jaw muscles.

Large canine teeth for catching and holding prey.

Streamlined body and camouflage fur coat.

Long slender limbs for running up to 28 mph.

Large flexible feet and sharp claws for gripping and climbing.

Large pointed ears and long, sensitive nose for tracking prey.

meaning it did not have rabies or another illness that might have caused it to attack.

Aside from the terror he experienced from having a wolf practically kill him, Zacariah was confused. He had heard many people, including his parents, say that wolves do not attack humans.

If this is the case, then how is it that Zacariah needed more than eighty stitches to close his wounds? His nose was broken in five places, part of his ear had been torn off, and his gums and cheekbone had been punctured. Zacariah describes his wolf attack as "the scariest night of my life."[2]

Zacariah was very brave. After the attack, he said, "Don't be scared to go into the woods: Don't think of wolves as killers. The chances of getting attacked are so slim; I can't get a hold of the fact that I was attacked. My parents were wrong when they said wolves don't attack people, but wolves almost never do."[3]

Why did the wolf attack Zacariah? According to reports, a wolf had been seen in the area for several days before the attack, doing everything from snatching backpacks and sneakers to eating human food. L. David Mech, a scientist who has studied wolves for forty years, believes the wolf had not only lost its fear of humans, but it had also been rewarded for it (by getting food and other items). Mech, who spent at least twelve summers living with and studying a pack of wild wolves, also suggests the possibility that the wolf was really interested in the sleeping bag, not Zacariah. Sound hard to believe? Mech reports that, like dogs, wolves like to play with fluffy or furry items. He says wolves have twice tried to take his sleeping bag–fortunately, two times when he was not in it. However, Mech comments, "while we need not return to the days when wolves were regarded as terrible demons, we do need to regard wolves with the respect due to any large animal."[4]

Scott Langevin's Mysterious Attack

Vargas Island Provincial Park, located on the west coast of Vancouver Island, Canada, was home to a pack of seven wolves. Campers, hikers, kayakers, and whale watchers enjoy Vargas Island. Twenty-three-year-old Scott Langevin was on a kayaking trip with some friends. One night, Langevin awoke to find a wolf tearing at his sleeping bag. Like Zacariah, Langevin had been sleeping outside of his tent.

Langevin yelled and kicked the wolf as it approached him. It backed off, but then attacked, biting Langevin through his sleeping bag. Fortunately, Langevin's friends heard the noise, and when they arrived on the scene, the wolf ran off. Langevin needed fifty stitches to reattach his scalp to his head and mend wounds to his hands and arms. After Langevin's attack, park officials recommended that all campers leave the island until they found the wolf responsible. Before long, they found four wolves. The animals fearlessly approached conservation officers. Two of the four were shot and killed.

Not Surprised

The attack on Scott Langevin was the first reported wolf attack in the area. But people who live on the island were not surprised. All seven Vargas Island wolves had become habituated by humans and even had been seen eating hot dogs out of people's hands as well as wandering onto people's porches.

It is easy to understand why wolves lose their natural fear of humans: The wolves realize that people are not dangerous and that they are a source of food. What scientists still have not figured out is why the wolves attack after behaving in a friendly and nonaggressive manner toward humans.

The wolf's sharp teeth make the animal a fierce hunter and dangerous predator.

Too Many Wolves?

Some scientists believe that too many wolves in one area may cause the attacks. An estimated 30 to 35 wolf packs live in Algonquin Provincial Park. Wolves number at about 300 in the spring and summer, when new pups are born, to about 150 in the winter. Some die, are killed, or leave the park for other areas. As the area has such a large number of wolves, it is possible that young wolves have a hard time finding their own territories. When they venture into campsites and find friendly humans with food, it is not hard to see why they might want to settle in the area. However, this still does not explain wolf attacks on people.

Since these incidents, Canadian park officials remind visitors how important it is to clean park areas of all food and trash and not to feed any wild animals. The government of British Columbia also raised the fine for feeding wildlife to three hundred dollars after the wolf attack on Scott Langevin. If people continue to feed wild animals, they are actually hurting them, not helping them. A wolf that is found wandering in campsites is likely to be shot to prevent a possible attack.

Child-Lifting Wolves in India

Reports of wolves carrying off and eating children in India date from as far back as the 1800s. In 1878 more than 600 people in India were killed by wolves. Most of the victims were children. Wolf attacks continue to be a serious problem today. Since the 1980s, at least 273 children in India have been attacked by wolves.

Eighty children were victims of wolf attacks between 1993 and 1995, in the Hazaribagh region of eastern India. Of the eighty victims, only twenty were rescued or survived. Five wolf packs were found to have been responsible for the attacks, which occurred in sixty-three villages. Almost all the children attacked were between three and eleven years old.

Wolf Attacks Increased

In 1996 the number of wolf attacks increased. Sixty-four children were seriously injured or killed by wolves in the north Indian state of Uttar Pradesh. Two scientists who studied these attacks suggested the possibility that one wolf was responsible. Wolves were reported to have killed more than fifty children in 1997 and injured several dozen more. Occasional attacks continued in 1998 and 1999.

The huge number of attacks by wolves in India is surprising, especially when compared to the small number of wolf attacks on humans in other areas of the world. No one knows for sure why so many attacks have occurred in this country, but scientists who have studied the problem have come up with several possible explanations.

Indian wolves today face a major problem finding food. Their natural prey is the antelope. People have hunted so many antelope in this area of India that the species has become extinct. As few prey animals are left, wolves have turned to livestock for food. In the communities where the people earn their living by herding and tending livestock, these animals are closely watched and protected from predators such as wolves and tigers. This makes hunting livestock difficult for the wolves.

Children in these **pastoral communities** are often allowed to wander outdoors by themselves while

Wolf attacks on children are common in pastoral communities in northern India (pictured).

A wolf chews on a tree branch. Wolves are known to lurk in the forests that surround northern India's rural villages.

their parents are tending the herds. Children often play in areas with high grass, which are easy places for wolves to approach without being seen. In Uttar Pradesh, where many wolf attacks occurred, scientists observed that children were allowed to play without adult supervision while livestock was carefully watched.

Rural Villages Allow Wolves to Hide

Conditions in the villages also make it easy for the wolves to enter areas where people live. Families in these rural villages live in huts. Like the wolves in the North American attacks, Indian wolves have become habituated to humans. It is common to see wolves in the villages, and they sometimes even enter people's huts. The huts have no bathrooms, so people must use the outdoors, often at the far edges of the village, as toilet areas. Wolves may be waiting in these areas.

The Indian government pays families whose children have been killed by wild animals. The amount of money paid to families is an amount larger than most people in the area earn in an entire year. Biologists who studied the Indian wolf attacks think that some children might purposely have been neglected. Their parents know that if anything happened to the children, the government would give them money.

It is still uncertain whether the 1996 attacks were the work of one wolf or several. The attacks occurred about every third day. The **puncture** wounds from the wolf's teeth examined on different victims were the same size. This could mean the same wolf attacked all the victims. Some wolf biologists believe one wolf was responsible for all sixty-four attacks in Uttar Pradesh.

A Predatory Pack

In 1997 another nine or ten children were killed in the same area of India. A ten-year-old girl named Manwati has scars that tell of the time a wolf snatched her from her bed and tried to eat her. Luckily, a man in the village heard Manwati cry out. When he went to see what was going on, the wolf dropped the girl and ran off.

In nearby villages other children were not so lucky. A five-year-old girl was taken by a wolf from the bed she was sleeping in with her mother, carried off, and eaten. A four-year-old boy was attacked and carried off by a wolf while outside his hut. His two siblings and his mother watched but could not save him.

In the 1997 cases a pack of wolves was believed to be responsible for the attacks. The wolves may have been starving. Habituation could have caused the animals to lose their natural **instinct** to avoid humans. These two reasons caused the wolves to see the children as prey.

The attacks frightened people in the villages. They wanted to do something to protect their families and neighbors. Thousands of villagers and police officers, armed with shotguns and long bamboo spears, hunted the wolves. The wolf hunts only resulted in ten wolves being killed, and it is not known if any of the animals shot were those responsible for the attacks.

Mysterious Explanations

This part of India is one of the poorest areas of the world, and most people have had little, if any, education. Indian children are raised on fairy tales much like the stories of "Little Red Riding Hood" and "The Three Little Pigs," which make them live in fear of wolves.

Not knowing the real reasons for the wolf attacks, people made up many stories, including tales that the attackers were really werewolves. Some people believed that humans dressed as wolves were to blame. They were thought to be people from the neighboring

Fairy tales such as Little Red Riding Hood and The Three Little Pigs (inset) can cause children to fear wolves.

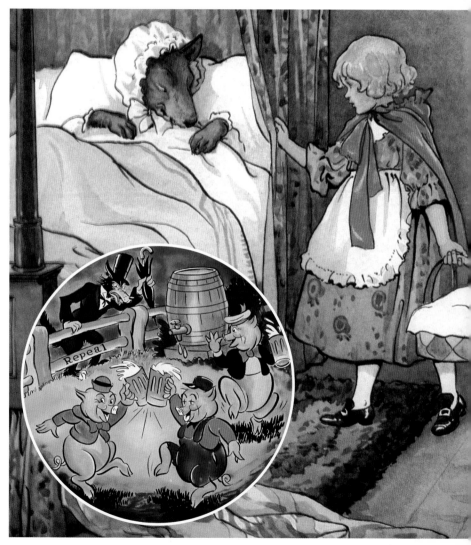

country of Pakistan. Pakistan and India have traditionally been enemies. The ten-year-old sister of a boy killed said of the wolf she saw take her brother, "It rose onto two legs until it was as tall as a man. . . . It was

A captive wolf sinks its teeth into a deer head. Starving wolves have been known to attack humans.

wearing a black coat, and a helmet and goggles." The grandfather of the same boy said, "We have seen this thing with our own eyes. It is not a wolf; it is a human being."[5]

In some cases, fear and anger caused people to fight with one another instead of working together to solve the wolf problem. These conflicts led to the deaths of twenty people as well as 150 arrests by police.

Preventing Attacks

Wolf experts and other people in India are working to try to solve this problem so more attacks will not occur. Further research on wolf behavior in India is necessary. This includes studying the places where wolves live and where packs gather, or **rendezvous**. Some biologists feel that limiting the number of wolves in an area is required. This may mean killing some wolves if it is believed there is not enough food for all of them. Another idea is to provide natural prey for the wolves. This means putting back, or re-introducing, herds of animals such as antelopes in areas where wolves live. If wolves depend on livestock for food and they cannot get these animals, a starving wolf certainly may attack a human as prey.

Watching young children carefully in areas where wolves live is very important. A hungry wolf that has lost its fear of humans can easily pick up a small child if it has the chance. If the attacking wolf lives in a pack, it is likely that other wolves will imitate this behavior if it results in getting food.

Chapter 4

Wolf Hybrids: Pets or Killers?

Most attacks by wolves on humans are by wolf-dog hybrids and captive wolves. Wolf-dog hybrids are animals that are part wolf and part dog. People keep wolf hybrids as pets for different reasons. Some people think owning a hybrid is like owning a wild wolf. They think it is cool to own something wild. Other people like having a pet that is unusual. Wolf experts agree hybrids can be dangerous to children and other animals. As with wild wolves, the majority of attacks by wolf hybrids have been on small children. Hybrids have even been known to attack children that they know and have played with many times.

The Beast of Gévaudan

Wolf hybrids have existed for hundreds of years. Attacks by these animals were recorded as far back as the 1700s. The most famous story of a hybrid attack comes from France. Between 1764 and 1767, the Beast of Gévaudan, or La Bête du Gévaudan, terrorized the French countryside. La Bête was responsible for killing at least sixty-four people and maybe as many as one hundred. At the time, some people thought the

An animal trainer sits next to a howling wolf hybrid. Like wild wolves, wolf hybrids have been known to attack people.

Beast of Gévaudan was a werewolf, and others thought it was a demon. A 1764 poster warning people to beware of the Beast described the animal as "reddish brown with dark ridged stripe down the back. Resembles wolf/hyena, but big as a donkey. Long gaping jaw, 6 claws, pointy upright ears and supple furry tail. . . . Cry: more like a horse neighing than a wolf howling. Last seen by people mostly now dead."[6]

In this painting, the fearsome Beast of Gévaudan pounces on a small child.

Under the king's orders, La Bête was hunted by many men, who used weapons, traps, and poisons. It was thought to have been killed on five separate occasions, but attacks continued after each. Finally, in 1767, a deformed wolflike animal was killed, and the attacks ended.

The story of the Beast of Gévaudan is so mysterious and gruesome that a 2002 horror film titled *Brotherhood of the Wolf* was based on it. Though it is not a well-known story in the United States, everyone in France has heard of La Bête. In France, the story of the Beast of Gévaudan has been called "the Greatest Enigma of History." An enigma is a mystery, or something that cannot be understood.

Solving the Mystery

According to C.H.D. Clarke, a Canadian naturalist who investigated the Gévaudan attacks, it is likely that there were two animals responsible, and they were probably wolf hybrids. This explains why attacks continued after they thought they had killed the Beast. At the time in France, huge dogs called mastiffs were often kept as guard dogs. It is quite possible that wolf-mastiff hybrids could be the size of the animals described by people and could be as aggressive, particularly if they had rabies. The two animals believed to be the killers weighed 130 pounds and 109 pounds, which is larger than any wild wolf in that area. Measurements of the animals' skulls proved that the animals were more dog than wolf.

A Deadly Combination

Wolf hybrid experts estimate that between three hundred thousand and five hundred thousand wolf hybrids live in the United States today. In recent years, stories of wolf hybrid attacks have appeared in the news. In Michigan, in 1990, two-year-old Tanya Elliot was killed by a wolf hybrid that belonged to a family friend whom she was visiting. The child had met the animal on other visits and had played with it without any problems. This time, Tanya's mother allowed her toddler to play alone in the backyard. The animal was kept outside, chained up. When they noticed the animal shaking something, they went outside to see what it was; it was Tanya. She had gone too close to the animal, and it had attacked her.

It is hard to believe something so horrible could happen right in someone's backyard. There were several very serious mistakes made and none were the fault of two-year-old Tanya. A young child should never be left alone with any animal, let alone one as unpredictable as a wolf dog. Wolf hybrid experts agree that hybrids should never be kept chained up because this can cause them to act more aggressively, which can lead to an attack.

A similar story was reported in Florida in 1988. A wolf hybrid had been adopted from an animal shelter. The same day it was brought to its new home, the animal escaped from its owner's yard. A neighbor found the animal and put it in her backyard while she tried to contact the owner. Her four-year-old son tried to play in the yard with the animal and was attacked and killed by it.

Another hybrid incident involved a wolf hybrid named Dakota who attacked a 10-year-old boy in a California supermarket parking lot. As he sat on the

A Big Paw

● How big is your hand compared to this life-size wolf hybrid paw?

curb eating an ice cream cone, the boy was grabbed by the animal and dragged twenty feet. Its owner said Dakota was just being playful and wanted some of the boy's ice cream. What makes this story more shocking is the fact that Dakota was used by its owner as part of his wolf wildlife education program, and was brought into classrooms to educate children about wolves. The 140-pound hybrid was reported to have jumped at a girl during a program at a high school and shredded her sweatshirt.

Unpredictable Behavior

Between 1979 and 1992 fourteen people in the United States were killed by wolf hybrids. Most of them were children. The behavior of the wolf hybrid is very unpredictable. Even if the animal has been friendly in the past, it may attack a person at any time.

Wolves and wolf hybrids commonly see human children as pups. In this case, the animals will generally act calm and friendly. But certain behaviors can cause a wolf or a hybrid to see a child as prey. Running, rolling on the ground, and yelling, all common to children playing, can appear as preylike behaviors to a wolf or a hybrid. In the wild, prey animals will run, fall down, or make loud noises when in danger of attack by a predator. The predator will then attack.

When people attempt to keep wolf hybrids indoors, the animals often destroy property such as furniture, doors, and walls. When kept outdoors, they will dig up the yard. Hybrids can dig a hole as deep

Although many people keep hybrids as pets, these animals can be dangerous to children.

as six feet. They often cannot be housebroken. Once they are no longer puppies, many owners find their hybrids too difficult to care for, even if they wanted a wolf dog when they first got it.

Sadly, there is no safe place for these animals. As they are known to be dangerous as pets, even most animal shelters will not accept hybrids. And because they have not been raised in the wild, hybrids that are released or abandoned by their owners into the wild generally do not survive. They do not know how to hunt for food, and they are not likely to be accepted by a wild wolf pack.

A hungry wolf leaps into the air to snatch prey from a tree. Although wolves usually avoid people, they will attack humans under certain conditions.

Conclusion

Wolves do not usually seek out humans as prey, but they are hunters, and under certain conditions, they can and will attack people. Wolves and wolf hybrids are capable of killing people.

To help avoid conflicts with wolves, do not leave food or garbage outside, do not feed any wildlife, and do not leave pets unattended outside. These simple actions can help save the lives of both humans and wolves. There is an expression, "a fed wolf is a dead wolf," which means that a wolf fed by humans will lose its natural fear of people and learn that hanging around areas where humans are offers rewards. In most places, any wolf reported to be wandering in areas that humans use, such as campsites, will be shot to avoid the chance of a person being hurt.

Most people will never see a wolf in the wild. There is a greater chance of getting killed by lightning, a car collision with a deer, or even a bee sting, than being attacked by a wolf. However, the small number of wolf attacks that do occur remind us that a wolf is a predator and an animal that should be respected for its ability to attack and kill.

Notes

Chapter 2: Wolf Attacks in North America

1. Quoted in *Northern Rockies Ambassador Wolf Program*, "Wolf Attack!" www.bitterroot.net.
2. Quoted in *Northern Rockies Ambassador Wolf Program*, "Wolf Attack!"
3. Quoted in *Northern Rockies Ambassador Wolf Program*, "Wolf Attack!"
4. Quoted in L. David Mech, "Who's Afraid of the Big Bad Wolf–Revisited," *International Wolf Center*, Spring 1998. www.wolf.org.

Chapter 3: Child-Lifting Wolves in India

5. Quoted in John Burns, "India Fighting Plague of Man-Eating Wolves," *New York Times*, September 1, 1996. www.natureswolves.com.

Chapter 4: Wolf Hybrids: Pets or Killers?

6. Quoted in Derek Brockis, "The Beast of Gévaudan." www.wolfcross.com.

Glossary

bounties: Rewards.

den: An enclosure in which wolf pups are born and where they spend their first few weeks of life.

extinct: No longer in existence.

firsthand: Direct.

habituation: The act of becoming used to something.

instinct: A behavior that an animal possesses from birth and does not need to learn.

pack: A group that gathers together to make hunting and other ways of surviving easier.

pastoral communities: Villages where the people make their living by raising and herding livestock animals such as cattle and sheep.

predator: An animal that hunts and kills other animals.

predatory attack: An attack by a predator on an animal for food.

prey: An animal hunted by another animal for food.

puncture: A hole made by something sharp.

rabies: A disease of warm-blooded animals that is caused by a virus and can be transmitted to a human by the bite of the infected animal; unless it is treated quickly it almost always causes death.

rabid: Condition of an animal that has rabies.

reintroduction: The act of putting an animal species back into an area where it once lived but has become extinct.

rendezvous site: A place where wolves gather.

sickle: A curved metal blade with a short handle.

wolfers: People who hunted wolves for money in the United States during the 1800s.

For Further Exploration

Books

Seymour Simon, *Wolves*. New York: Scholastic, 1993. This book explains the behavior and habits of North American wolves. It explores the ways in which wolves raise their young, hunt for food, and work together in their packs. It has beautiful photographs of wolves.

Bruce Weide and Patricia Tucker, *There's a Wolf in the Classroom*. Minneapolis: Carolrhoda, 1995. This book tells the true story of Koani, a gray wolf, and Indy, a dog, who are wolf ambassadors who go to schools to teach students about wolves. The book also discusses why wolves do not make good pets.

John Zeaman, *How the Wolf Became the Dog*. New York: Franklin Watts, 1998. This interesting book explains how dogs became domesticated from wild wolves and the history of dogs and their relationships with humans. It has great photographs of wolves and various breeds of dogs.

Websites

International Wolf Center (www.wolf.org). The International Wolf Center is an organization whose goal is to teach the world about wolves. The center's website offers information about wolves, including tips on avoiding conflicts with wolves and articles on wolf attacks and wolf-human interactions in Canada and Alaska.

Timber Wolf Information Network (www.timber wolfinformation.org). This website provides links to articles about timber wolves, other types of wolves, wolf-human conflicts, wolf populations around the world, and many other topics. It also has a children's page.

Video

Jim Dutcher, *Wolves at Our Door*. Santa Monica, CA: Family Home Entertainment, 1997. This fascinating video is about Jim and Jamie Dutcher, who lived with a pack of grey wolves for three years in the American Northwest.

Index

Picture Credits

Cover: © Terry W. Eggers/CORBIS
© AP/Loveland Daily Reporter-Herald, 37
© Associated Press/AP, 10, 31
© Jim Brandenburg/Minden Pictures, 7
COREL Corporation, 14 (both), 23 (both)
© Michael DeYoung/CORBIS, 5
© David J. & Janice L. Frent Collection/
    CORBIS, 27 (inset)
© Will Higgs, 16 (inset)
Image Club, 27
Chris Jouan, 9, 16, 35
© Mary Evans Picture Library, 32
© R.P.G/CORBIS SYGMA, 15
Sir Peter Paul Rubens/COREL Corporation, 6
© Monty Sloan/www.wolfpark.org, 19, 24, 28, 38

About the Author

Elizabeth J. Scholl is a writer of children's books and educational materials. She lives in Hillsdale, New Jersey, with her husband, three children, and dog. When she is not writing, Elizabeth enjoys gardening, bicycling, and watching wildlife.